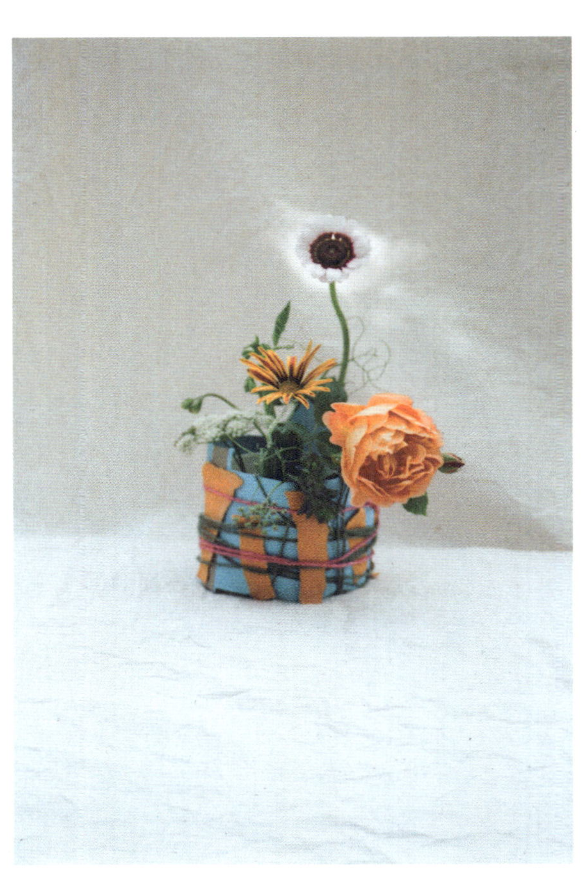

3

4

We are pleased to present *Dreaming About Tomorrow*, a solo exhibition of works by UK-based artist Johanna Tagada Hoffbeck. The exhibition features new paintings, some in oil, others using natural pigments, including some created from plants grown in the artist's allotment. Photographs from her ongoing series *Analog Diary* and unique collaborative works with ceramic designer Olivia Fiddes (UK) and weaver Pauline Simonet (France) will also be on view. In addition, a *Seed Library* will be set up within the exhibition site as an activity of *The Gardening Drawing Club*, a not-for-profit endeavour established by the artist in 2021. Tagada Hoffbeck has been actively invited to hold exhibitions throughout Europe and Asia. *Dreaming About Tomorrow* will be her third solo exhibition at the gallery. We hope that you will enjoy your visit.

5

この度Nidi Galleryでは、イギリスを拠点に活動するアーティスト、ジョアンナ・タガダ・ホフベックの個展「*Dreaming About Tomorrow*」を開催いたします。本展では、新作の油彩画や自身の農園で育てた植物などから採取した天然の絵具による絵画を中心に、プロジェクト「アナログ・ダイアリー」から写真作品、セラミックデザイナーのOlivia Fiddes(オリヴィア・フィデス/イギリス)、織物作家のPauline Simonet(ポリーン・シモネ/フランス)とのユニークな共同作品などを発表いたし

ます。また、会場には、昨年彼女が始めた非営利の取り組み「*The Gardening Drawing Club*」の活動として、どなたでも参加できる「シードライブラリー(種の図書館/種の交換ボックス)」を設置します。ヨーロッパ、アジア各地で精力的に展覧会を開催するタガダ・ホフベック。当ギャラリーでは2年ぶり3度目の個展となります。ぜひこの機会にお越しください。

A Message by Johanna Tagada
Hoffbeck

Dreaming about tomorrow. This might seem like a strange title, an odd encouragement given the current world situation, with crisis talks around climate change, life postpandemic and continuing warfare etc. Yet, this is what I invite you to do. To think positively about tomorrow, the day after, and those that follow – dare to dream. The title of this exhibition originated in 2019, whilst discussing ideas for future collaborations with Nidi Gallery. Unexpectedly, my dear grandmother, Yolande, passed away. A sudden and unimaginable suicide. Those who have known my work for some time might have sensed how close we were; she was a teacher, a friend and to some extent, a mother. For months, I was existing in a highly fragile state of being. Slowly, slowly with support and nourished by gardening, I dreamt of tomorrow again, which is why I now feel comfortable enough to write these words, hoping to encourage others to dream (again) too. The course of my life and

6

work has become more evident since 2020. I began studying social and therapeutic horticulture, engaging in further learning to build upon the legacy inherited via my family's involvement with permaculture. I currently live in the Oxfordshire countryside with my husband, where I spend almost as much time in gardens as I do in my studio. My interests in kindness, togetherness, compassion and community have developed much further, as I now organise and facilitate multiple workshops fusing arts with horticulture. My desire to encourage and nurture joy and compassion and to help alleviate the suffering of all of nature, has manifested via *The Gardening Drawing Club*. When visiting this exhibition, I hope that you may experience some of the energy I feel when gardening and enjoying green spaces with others; a sense of curiosity, wonder and enthusiasm for the months and seasons ahead. Each time I plant a seed, I do not fear the future but look forward to it. When I dream of tomorrow, I dream of sitting in my atelier close to Jatinder, painting gardens and people in them for a lifetime. I dream of a world where humans will no longer slaughter animals. I hope that we will endeavour to collaborate and form this kinder world together.

『明日を夢みる』－気候変動、（ポスト）パンデミック、戦争と今の状況を考えると、この展覧会タイトルは、奇妙な励ましに聞こえるかもしれない。それでもこれが今回みなさんと一緒にやりたいこと。明日、明後日と続いていく日々を、明るく想い描くこと。夢みること。今回の展覧会タイトルの由来は、Nidi Gallery と実現したい共同プロジェクトのアイディアを話していた2019年に遡る。私の大好きな祖母ヨランドが、突然亡くなった。突然、想像もしていなかった、自殺という形で。私の作品をしばらくの間見続けている人達は、作品から私と祖母の親密さを感じていたかもしれない。祖母は、私にとって先生であり、友人であり、ある意味母であった。何ヶ月もの間、私はとても壊れやすい状態にあった。ゆっ

くり、ゆっくりと、ガーデニングの助けを借りて、回復していった。私はまた明日を夢みるようになったのだ。だからこそ今、私はごく自然な気持ちでこの言葉を書き、他者が再び夢みることを励ますのだ。私の人生と仕事は、2020年以来、はっきりとした形を持ち始めている。社会学的心理学的なアプローチの園芸を学び始め、家族が代々携わってきたパーマカルチャーではなく、園芸を深めていこうと決心した。現在、オックスフォードシャー市の郊外

8

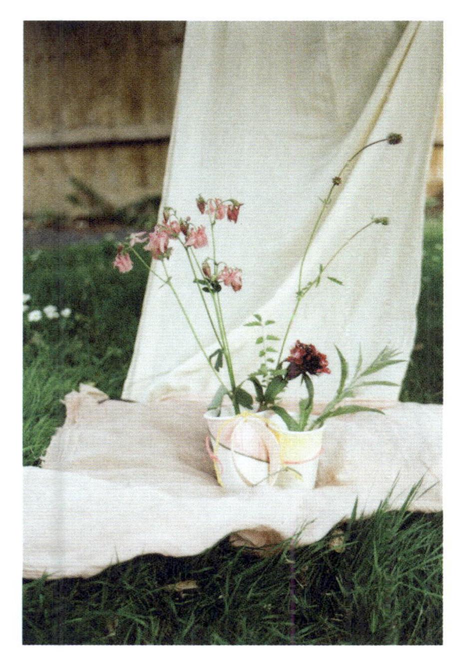

に夫と暮らし、スタジオで過ごす時間と同じくらい多くの時間を庭で過ごしている。私の個人的な興味であった、優しさ、連帯、思いやり、コミュニティーというテーマは大きく発展し、今では、アートと園芸をテーマにしたワークショップを企画し運営している。励ましたい、喜びを育てたい、共感したい、全ての生

き物の苦しみを緩和したい、という私の願いは、ガーデニング・ドローイング・クラブのマニフェストとなっている。この展覧会を訪れたあなたが、私がガーデニングをする時、誰かと一緒に庭にいる時に感じるエネルギーを少しでも感じてくれたら嬉しいです。それは好奇心であり、不思議に思うことであり、数ヶ月先や次の季節を待ち望むこと。種を植えるときはいつでも、将来に不安を覚えることなく、ただた

だ楽しみに思うのです。明日を夢みるとき、私はジャティンダーの近くに座って、庭や庭にいる人々を一生描いていくことを夢みます。私の夢は、人間が動物をこれ以上殺さない世界が訪れること。そういう優しい世界を共に作れるようになることを望みます。

9

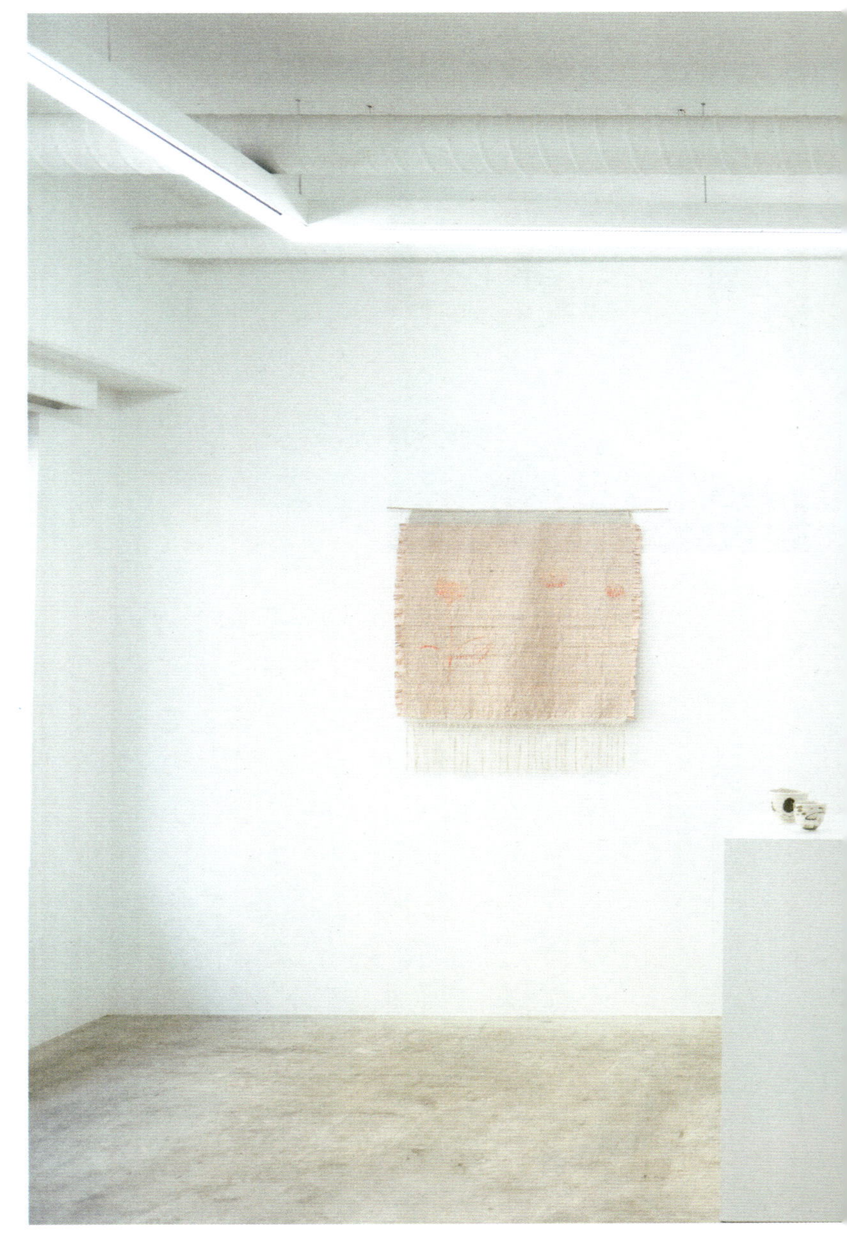

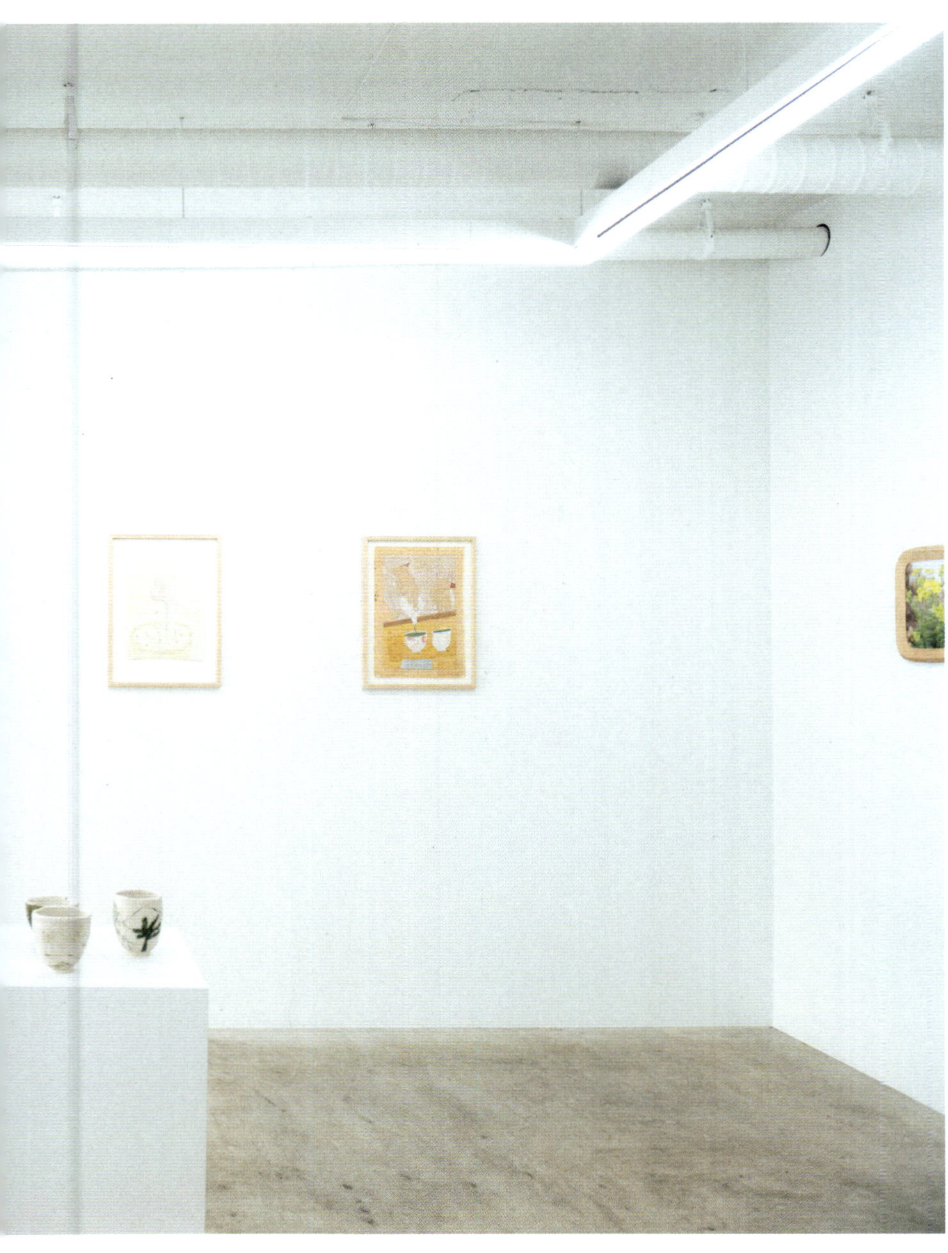

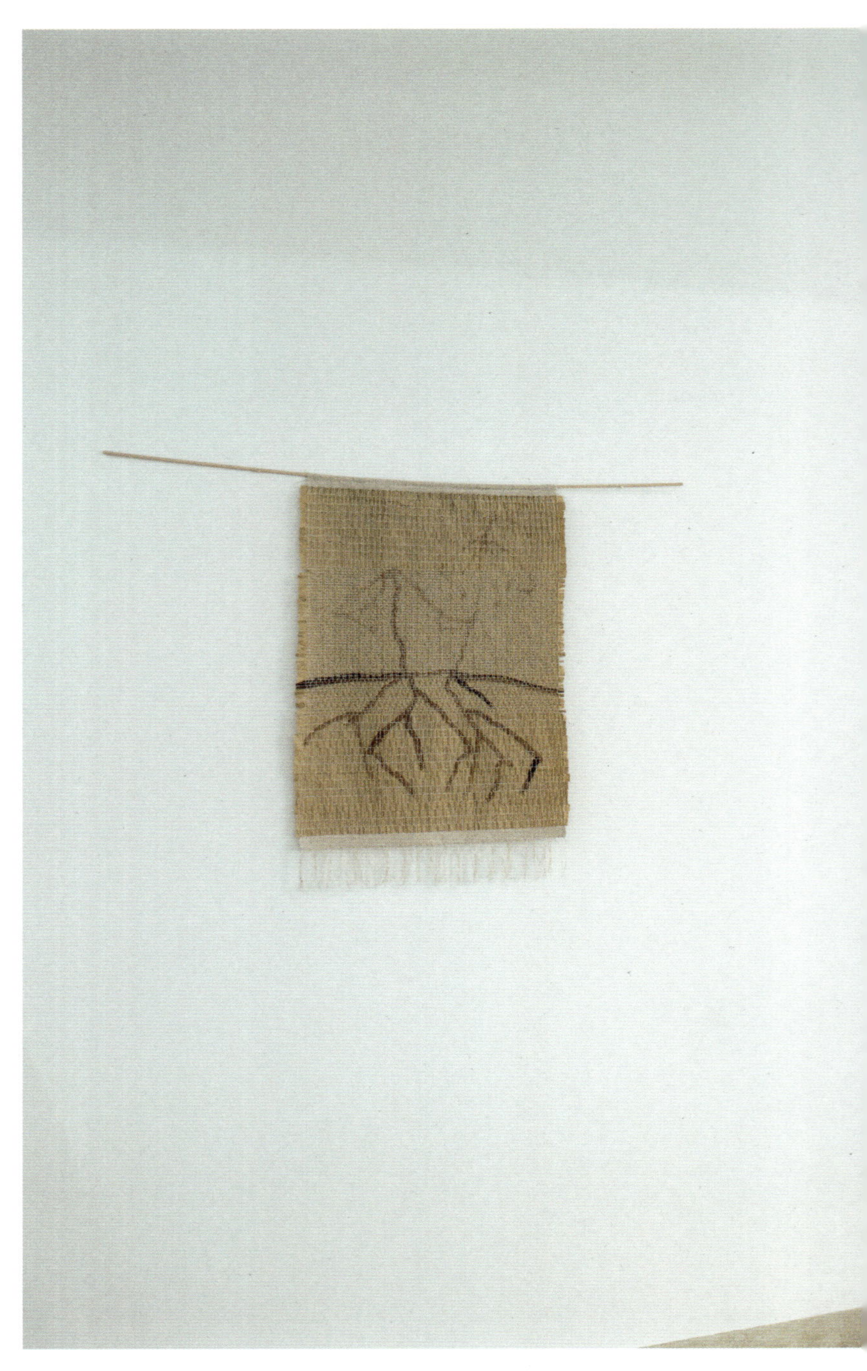

12

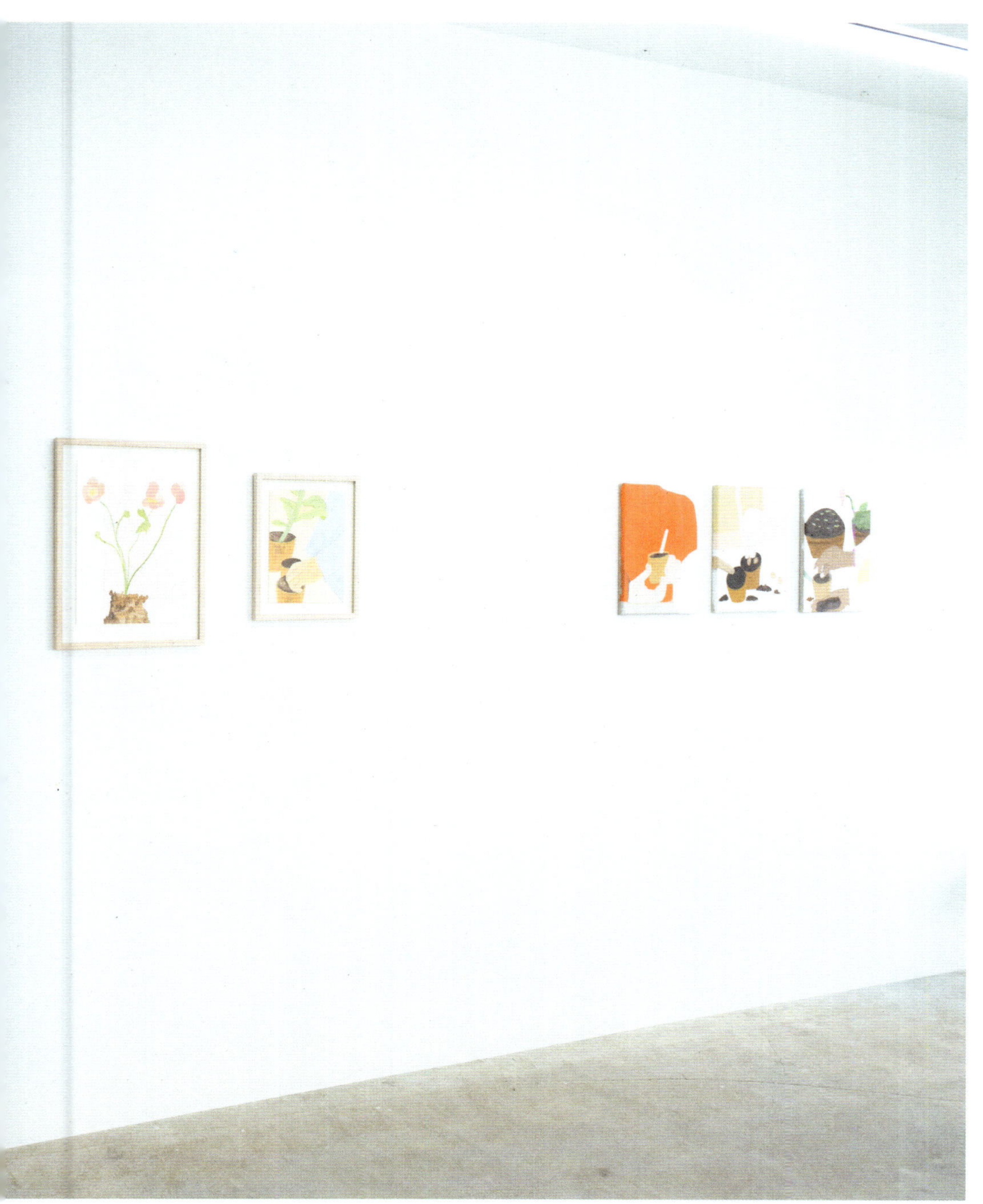

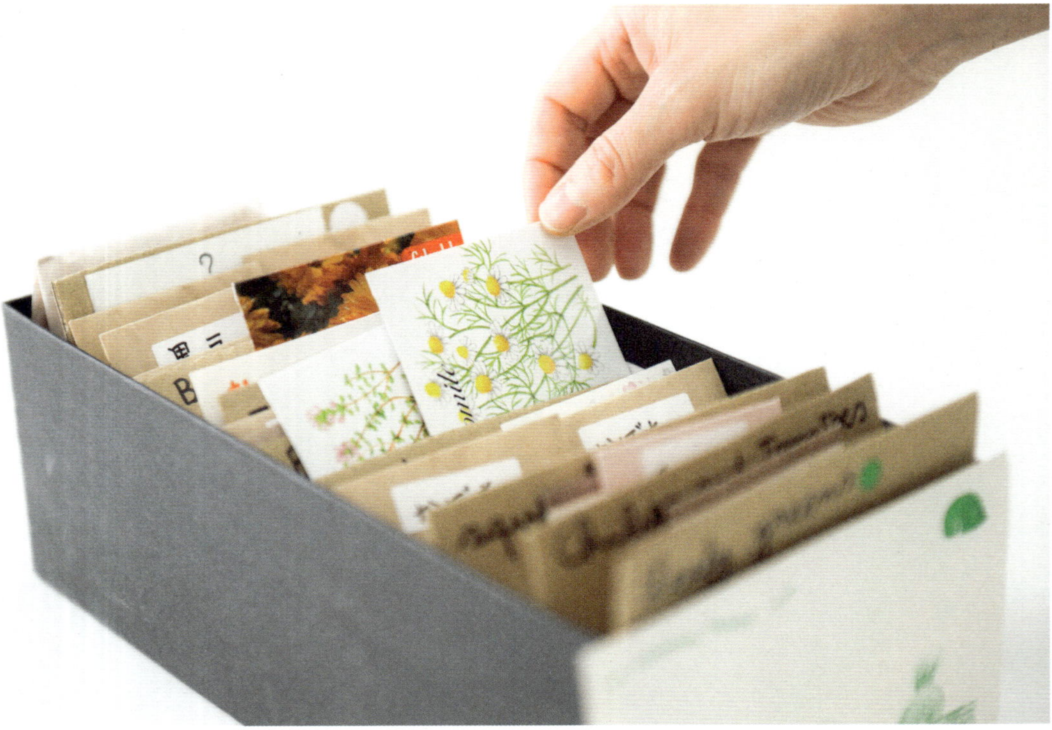

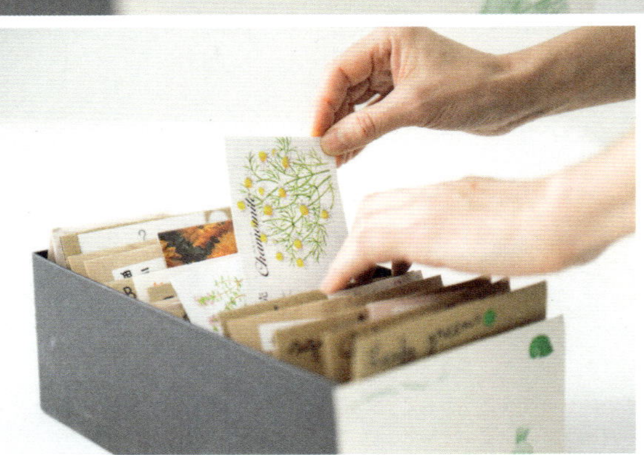

14

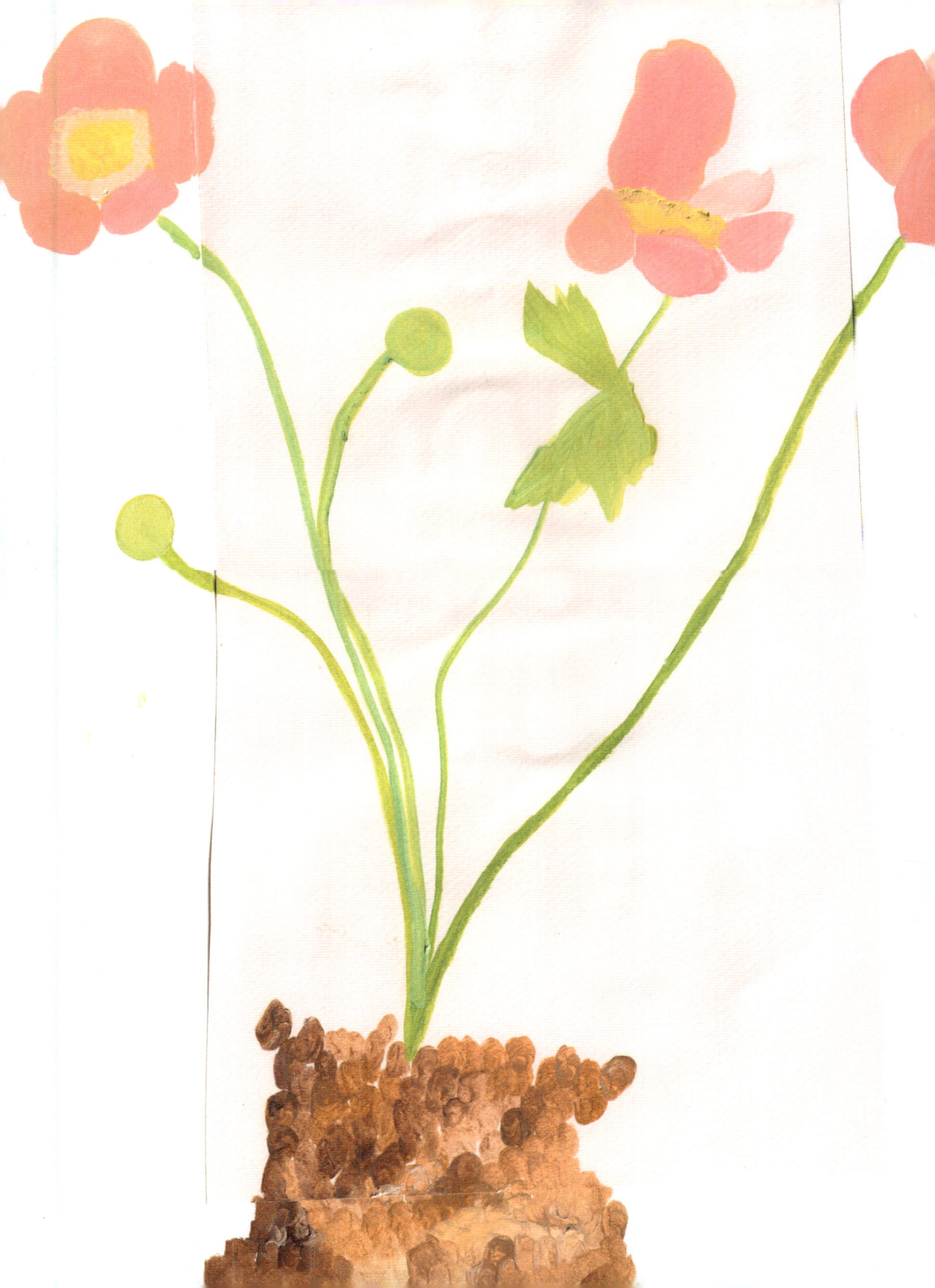

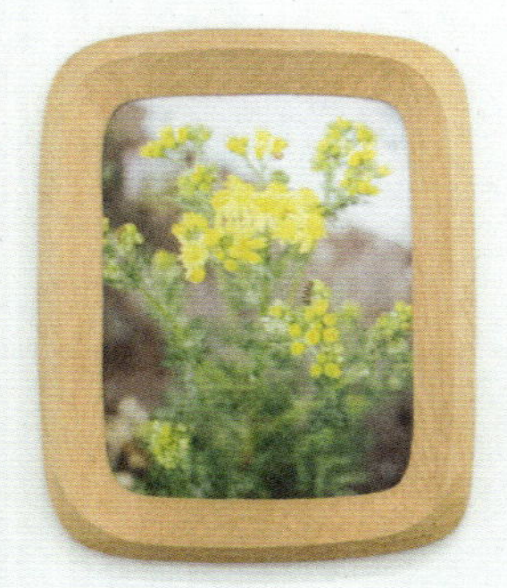 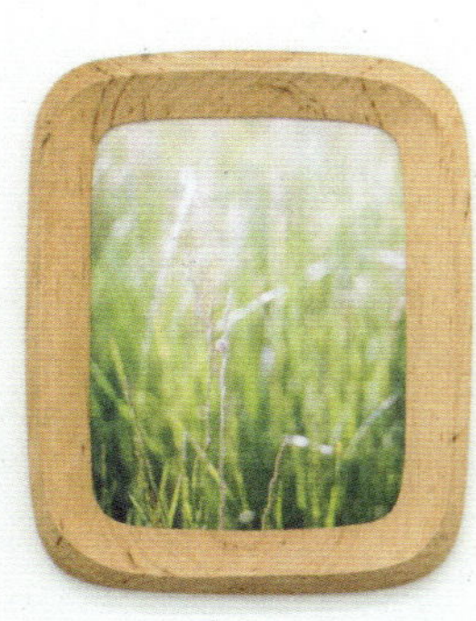

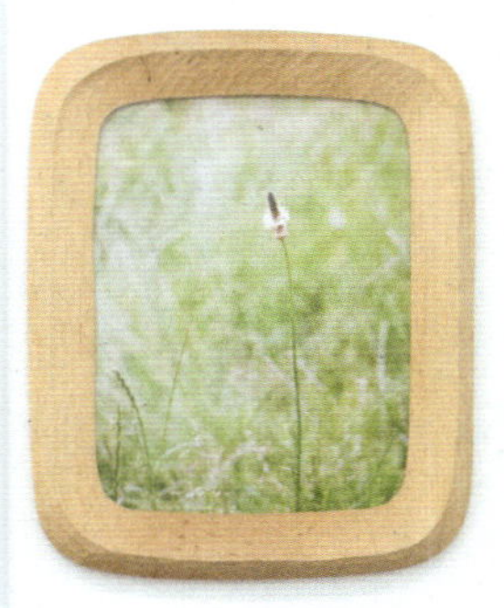
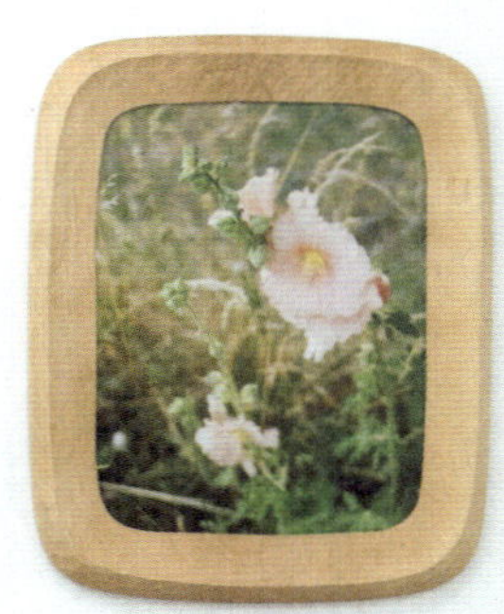

17

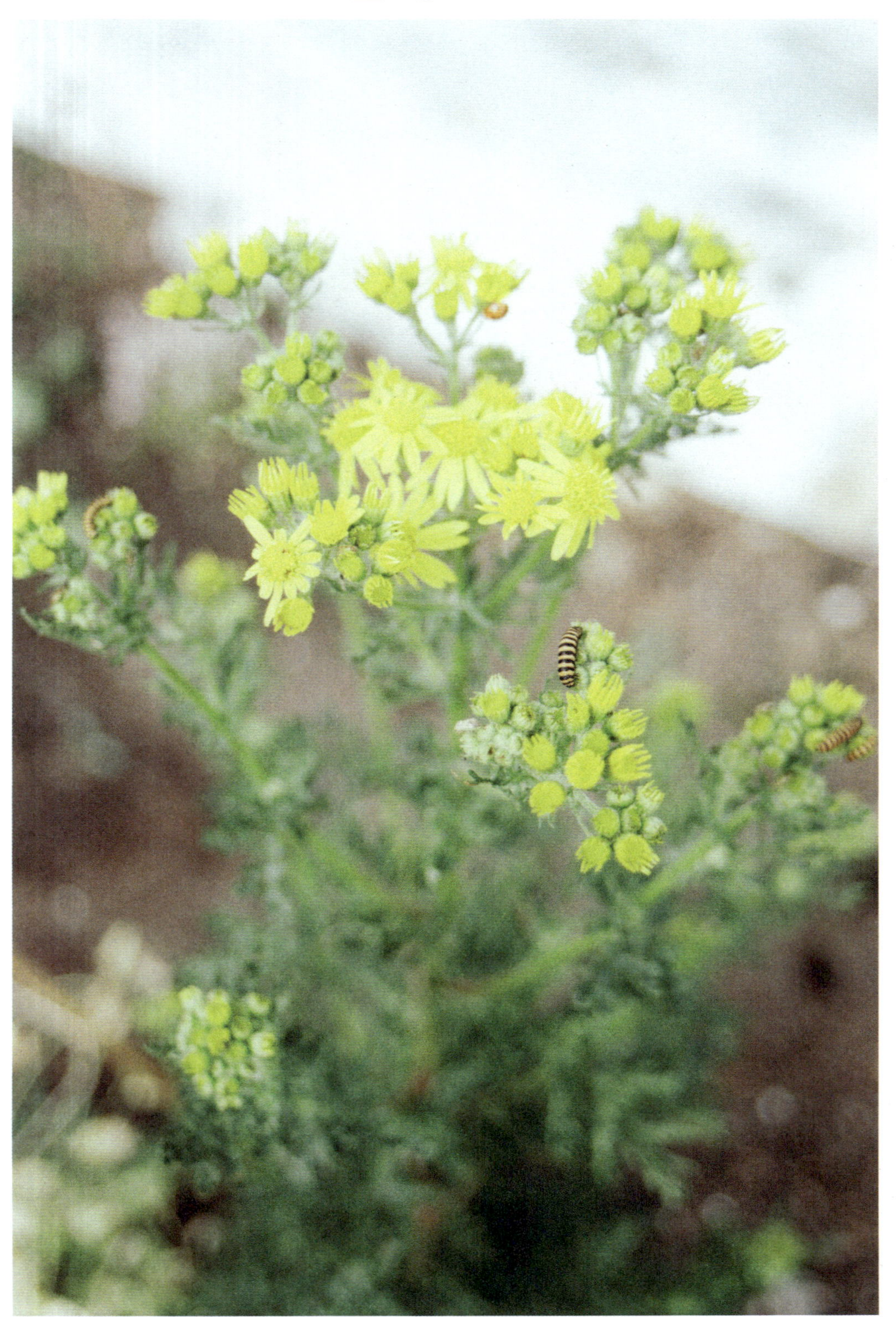

20

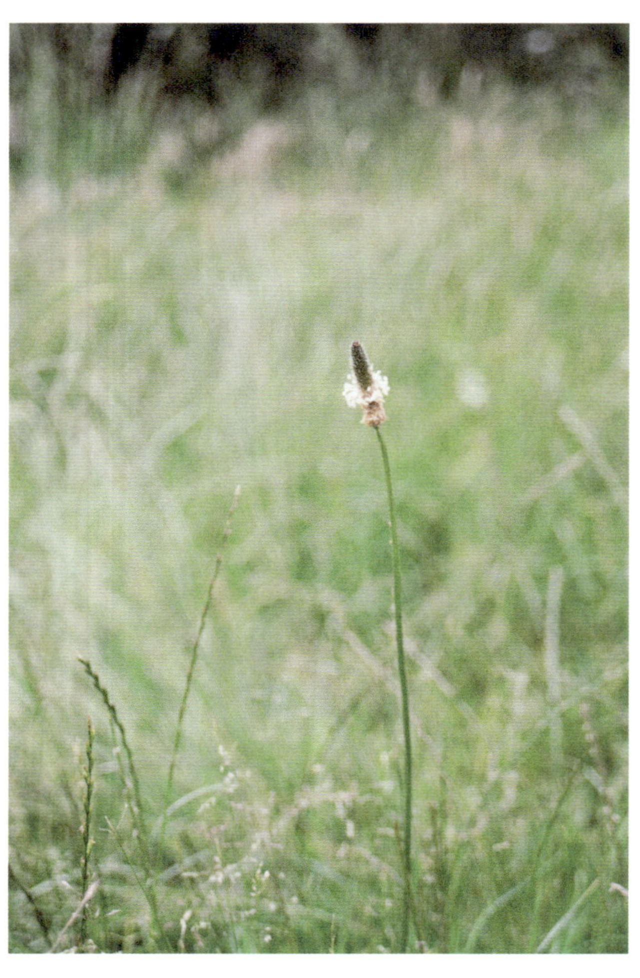

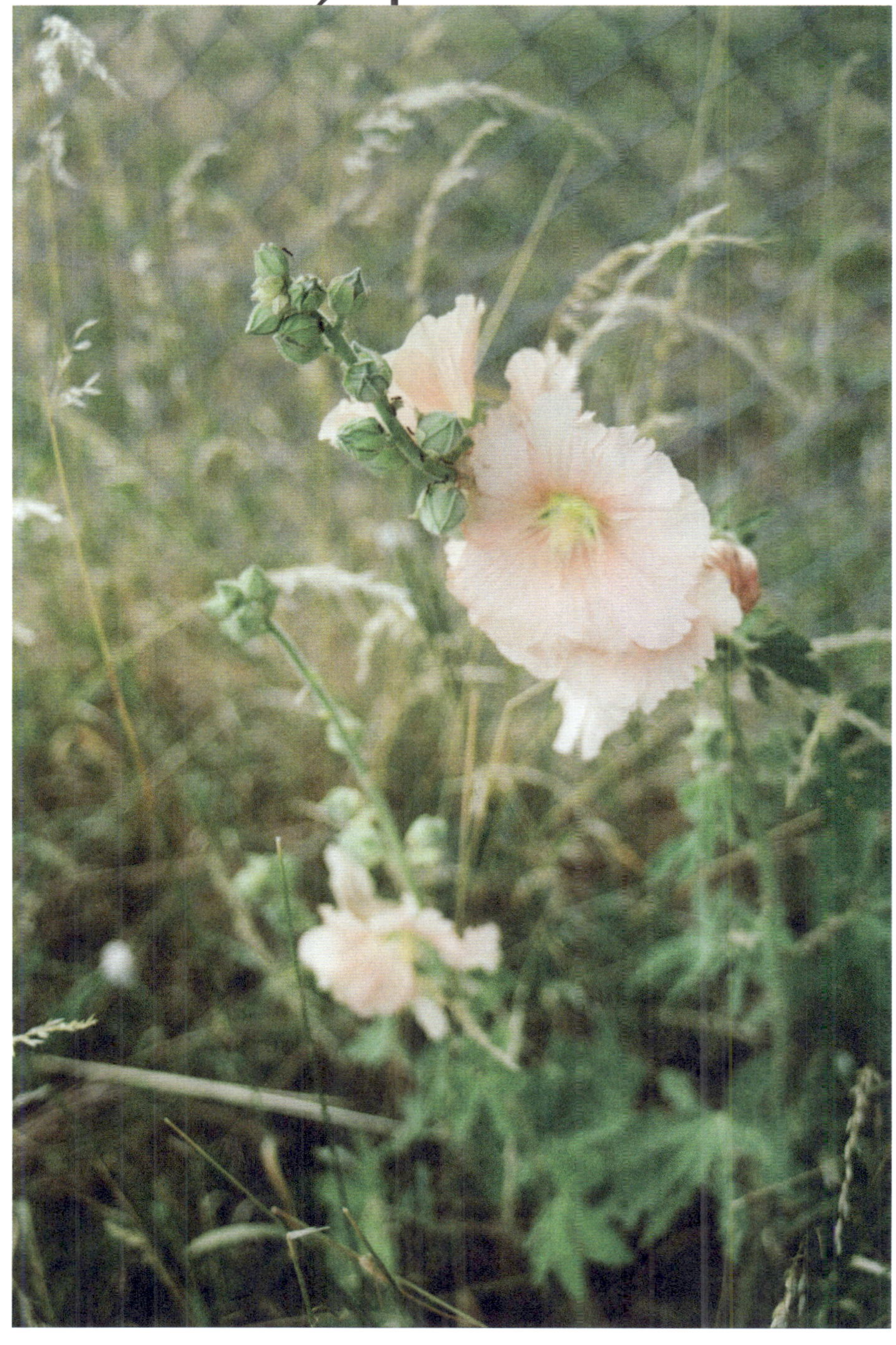

22

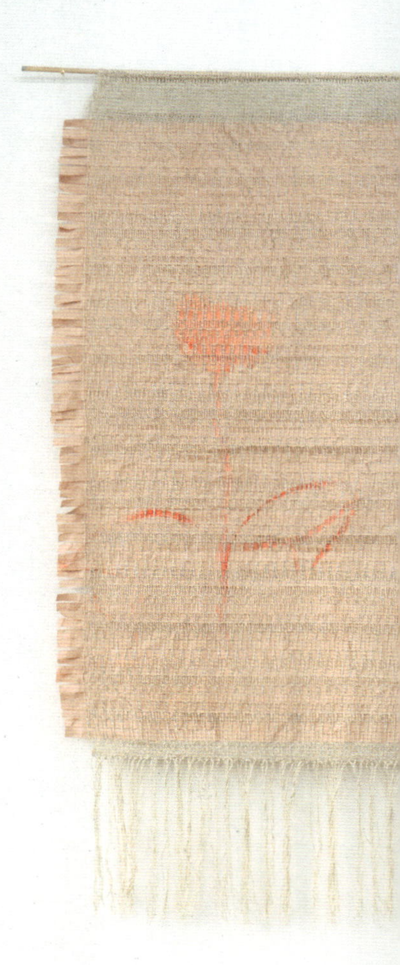

23

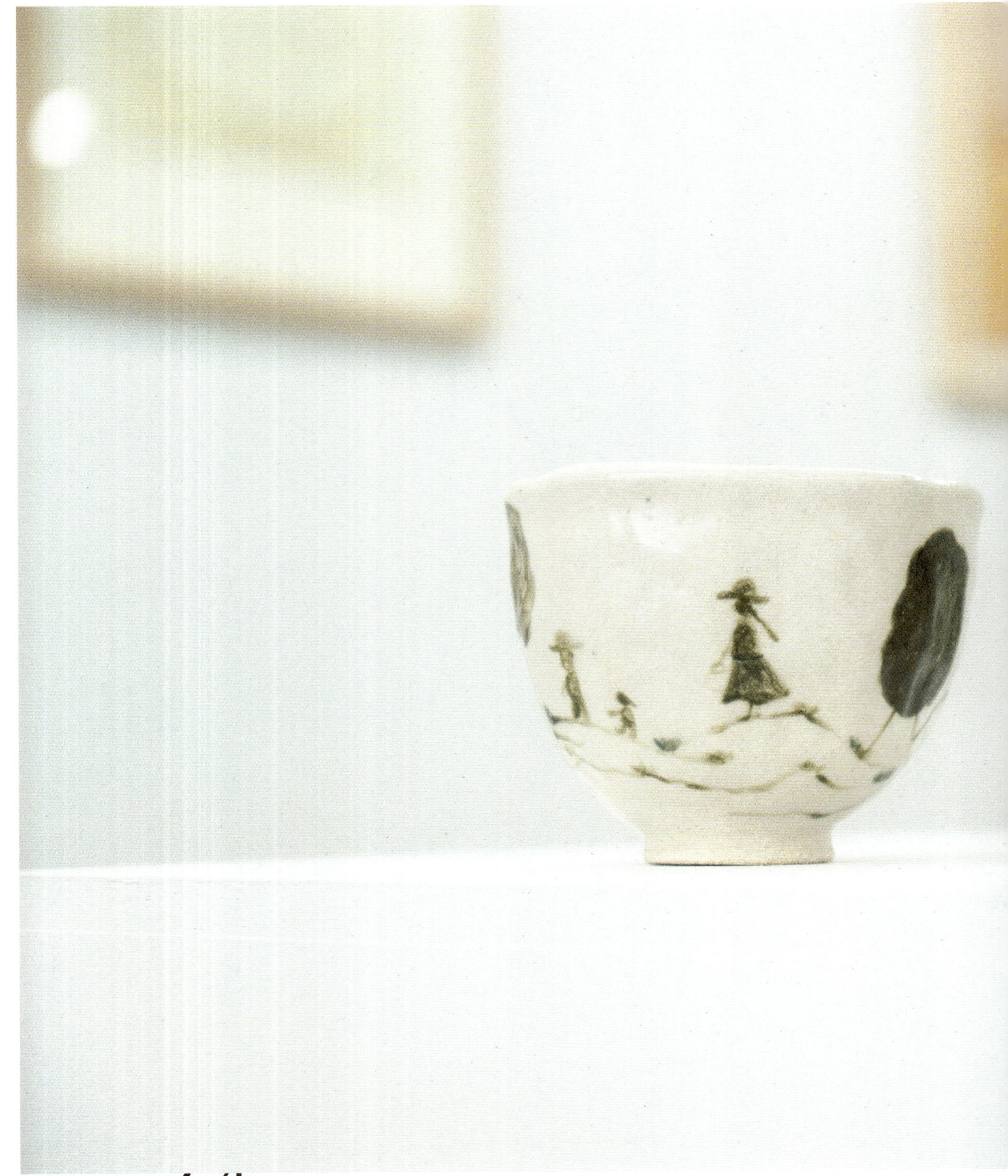

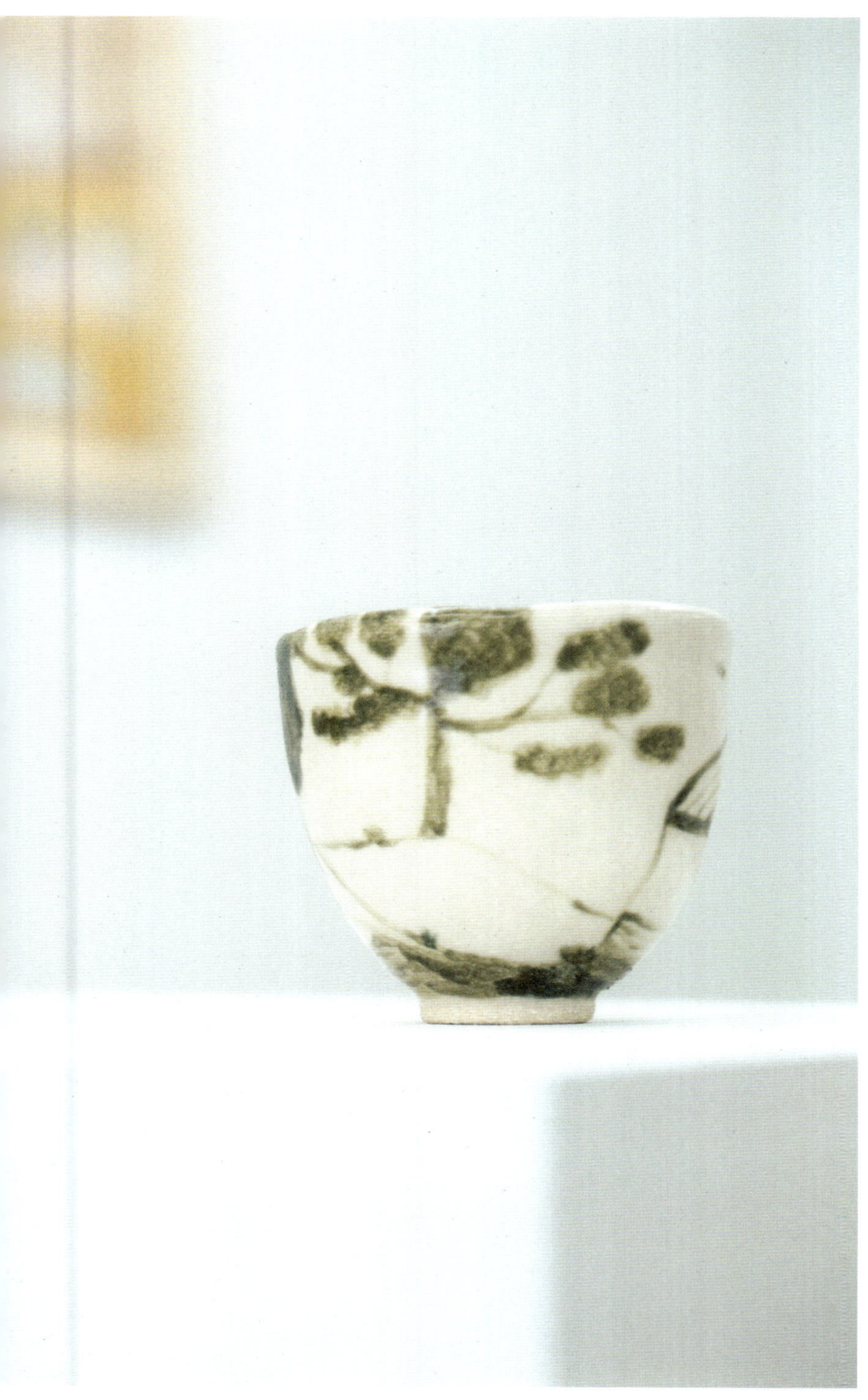

25

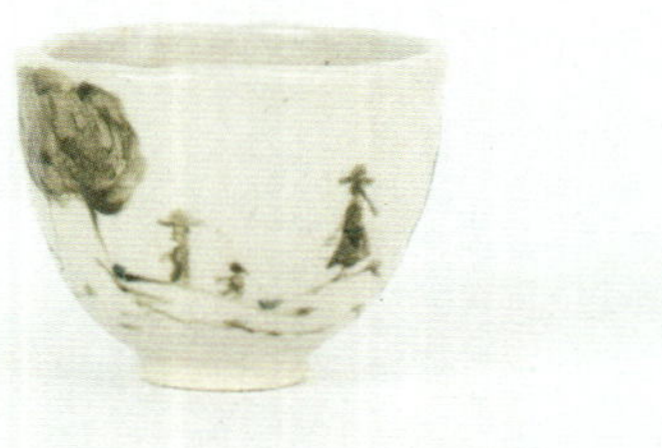
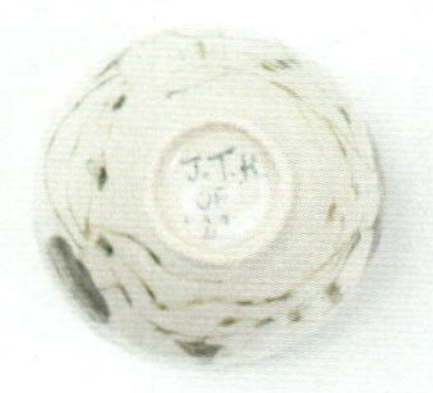
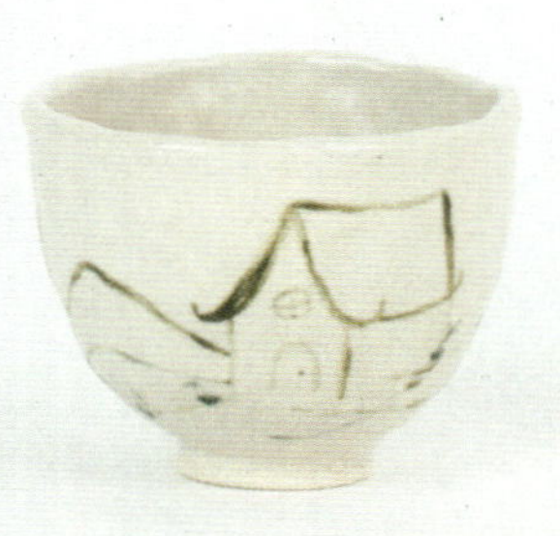
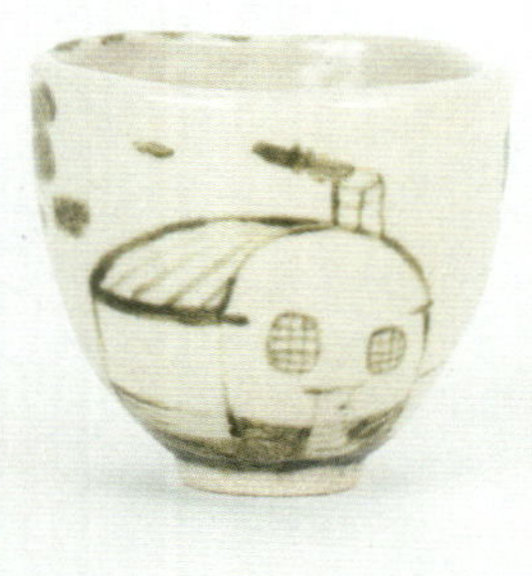
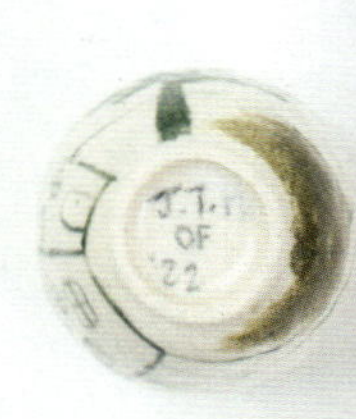

26

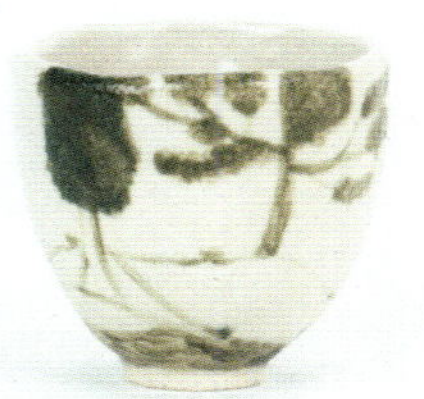
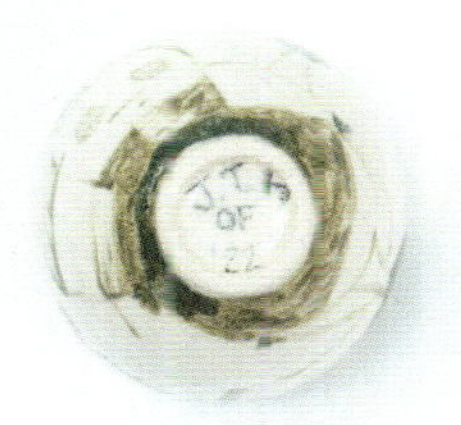
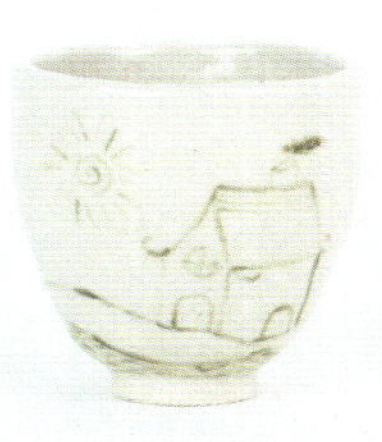
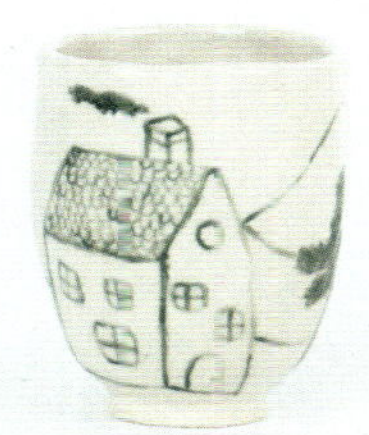
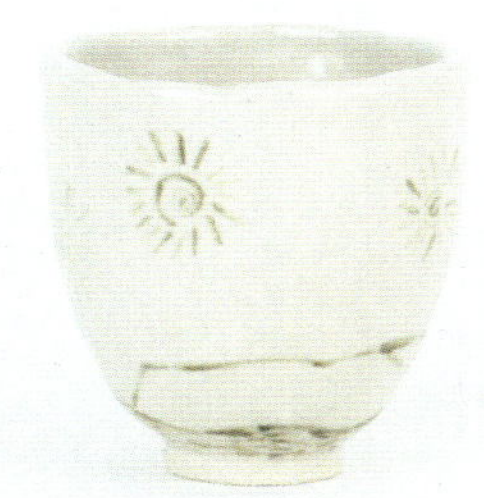
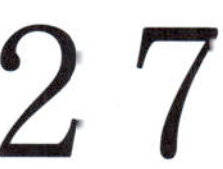
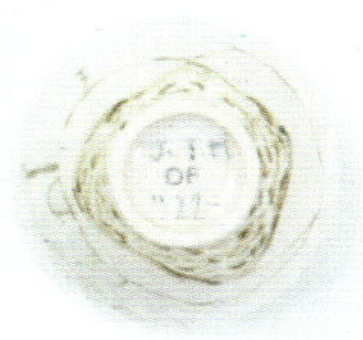
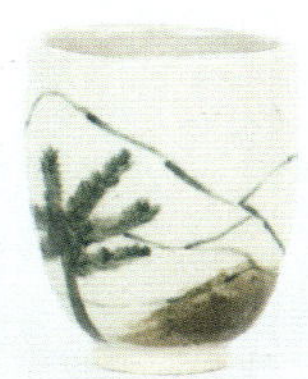

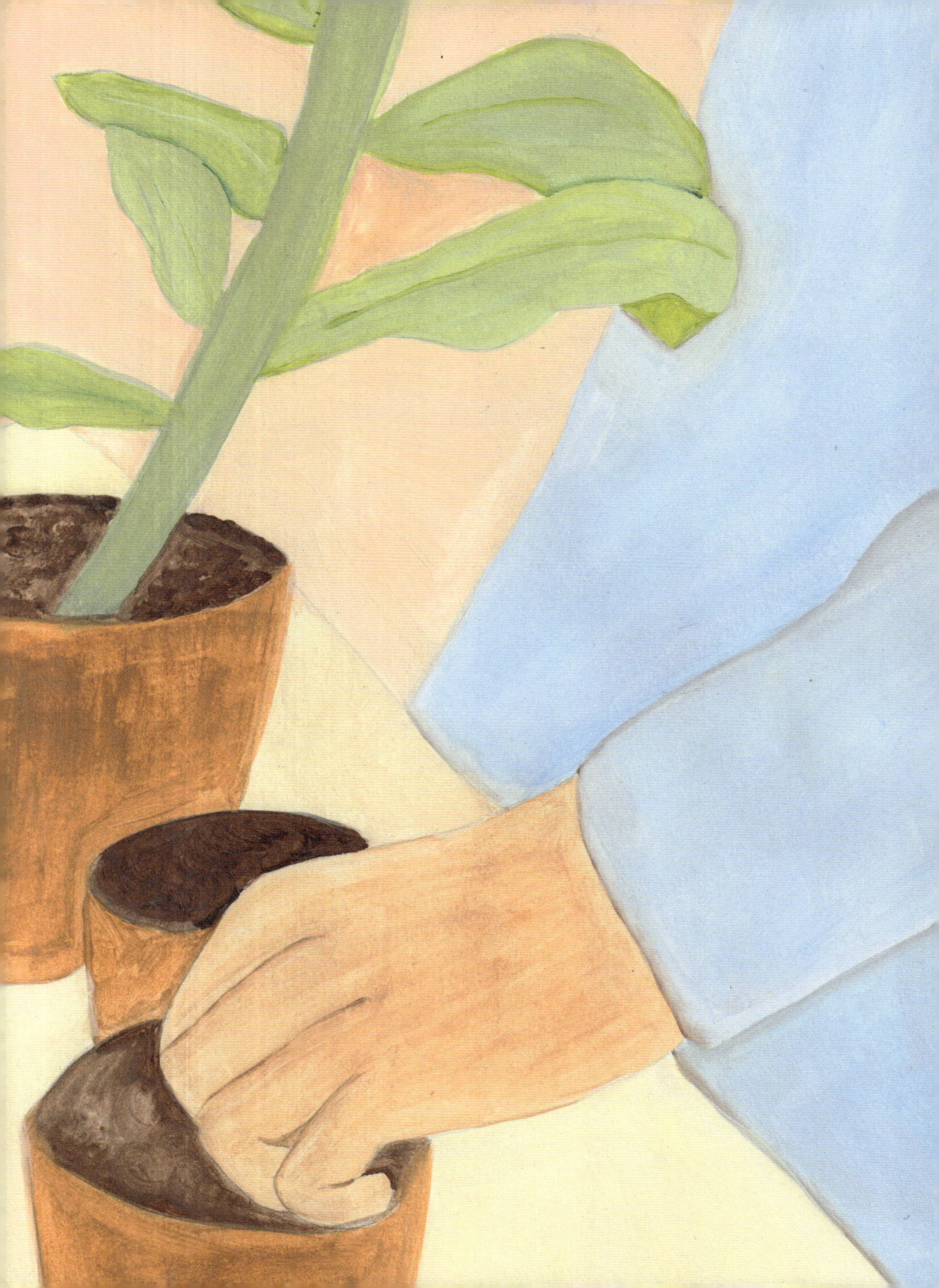

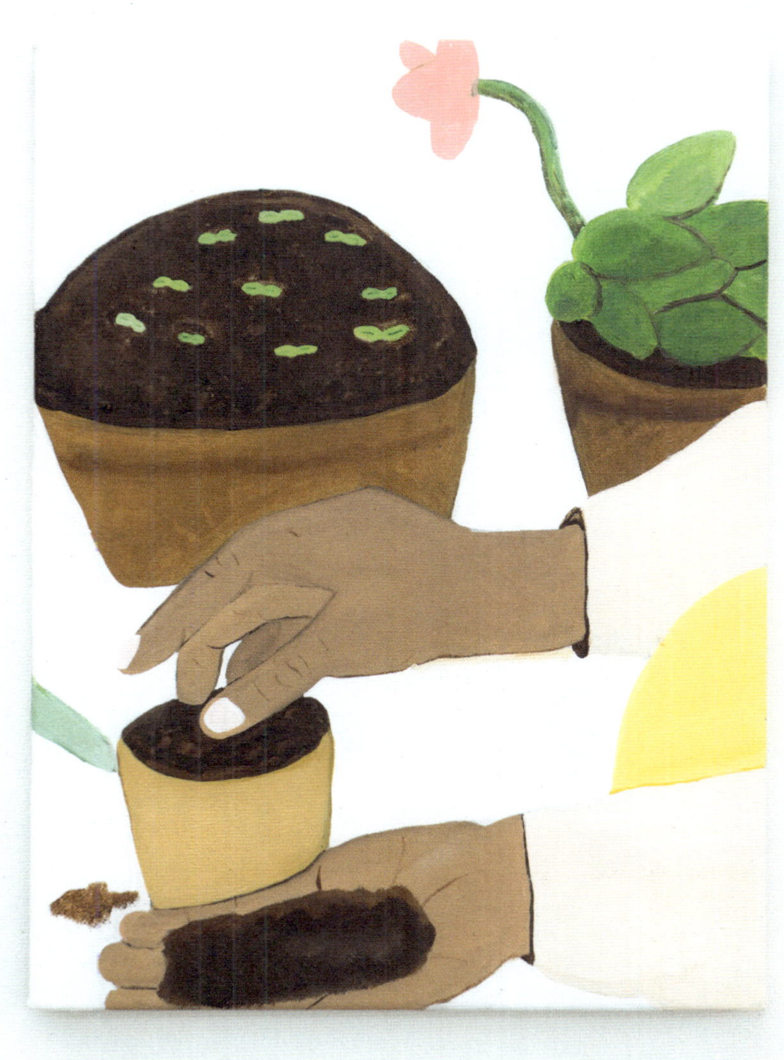

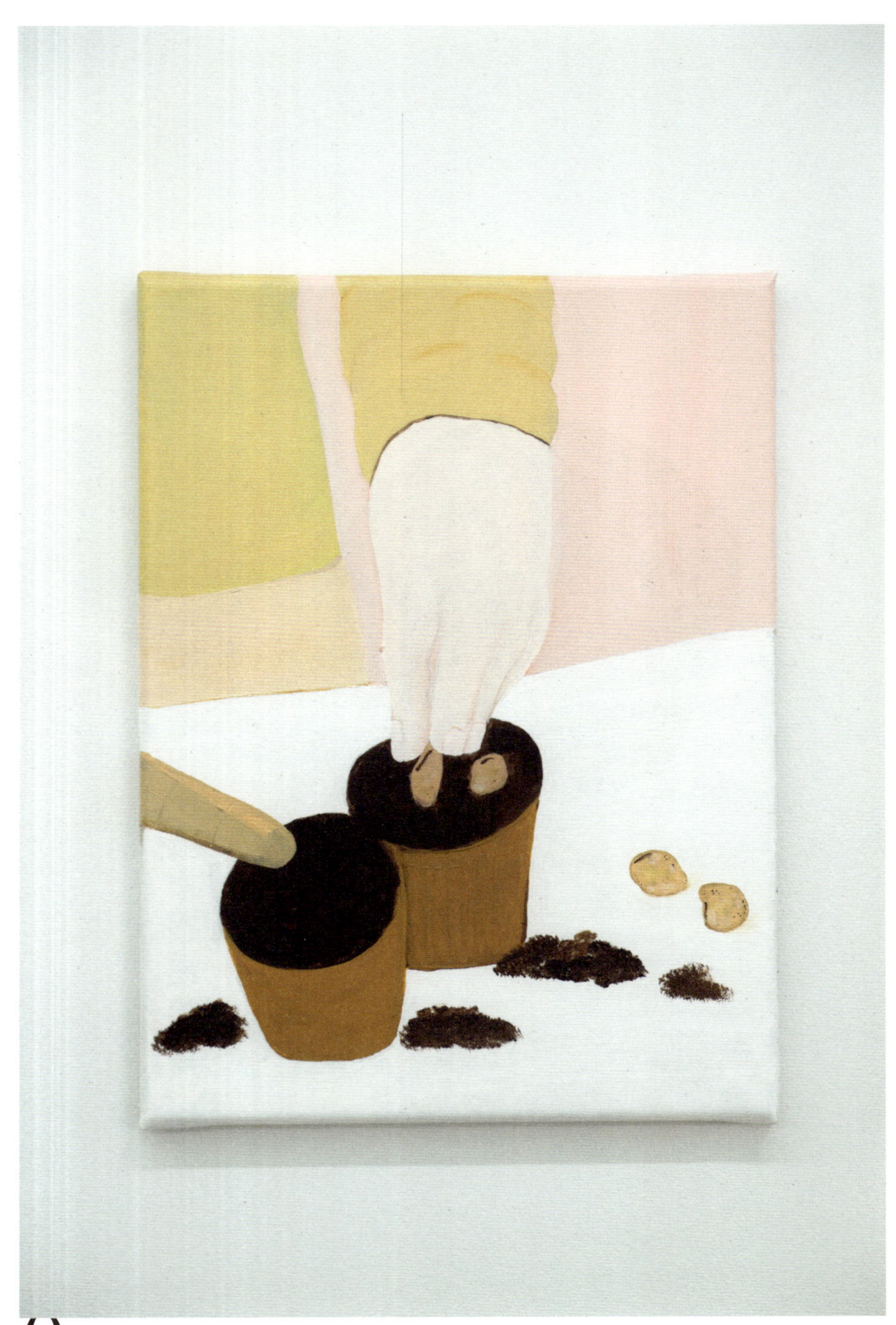

30

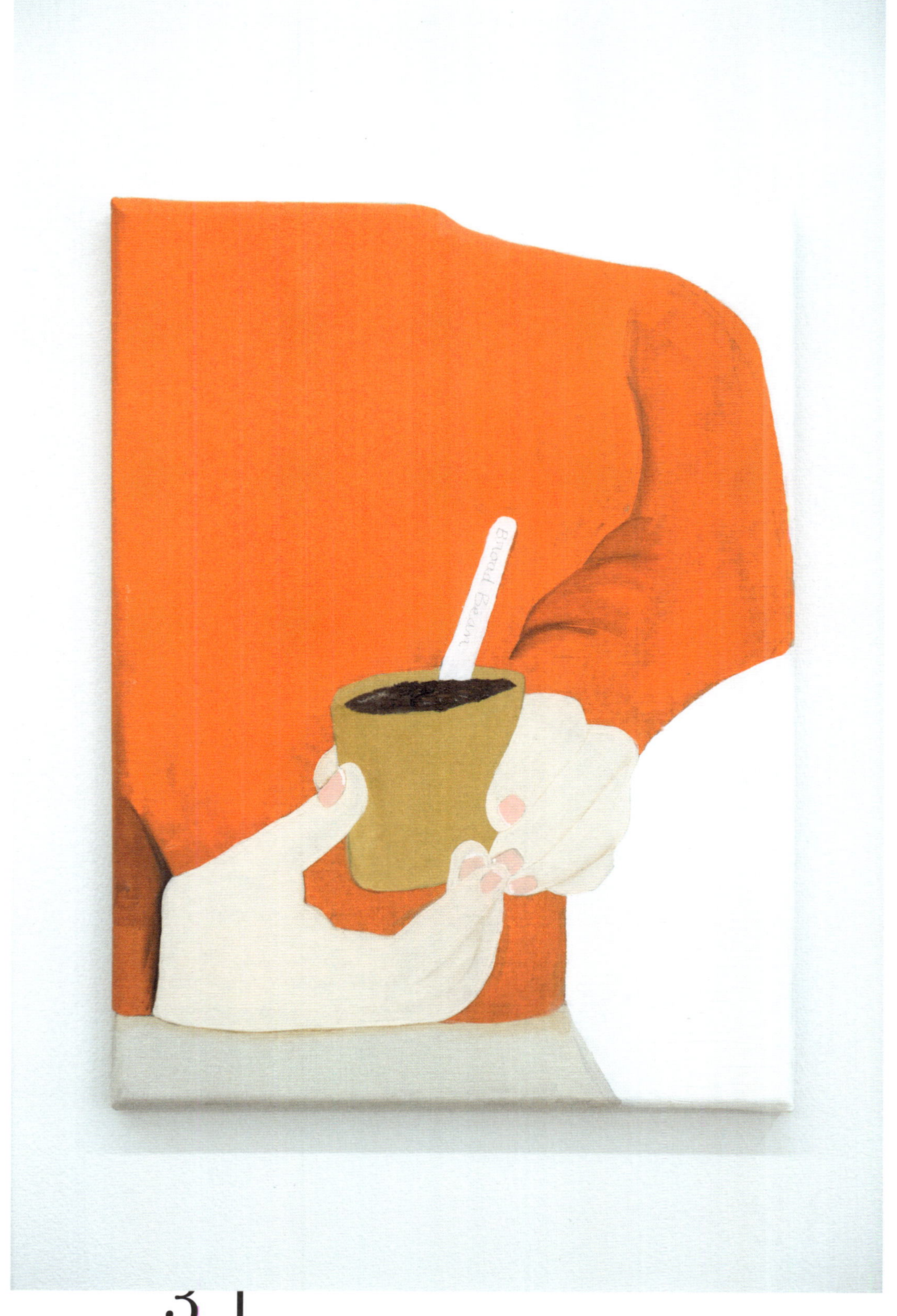

31

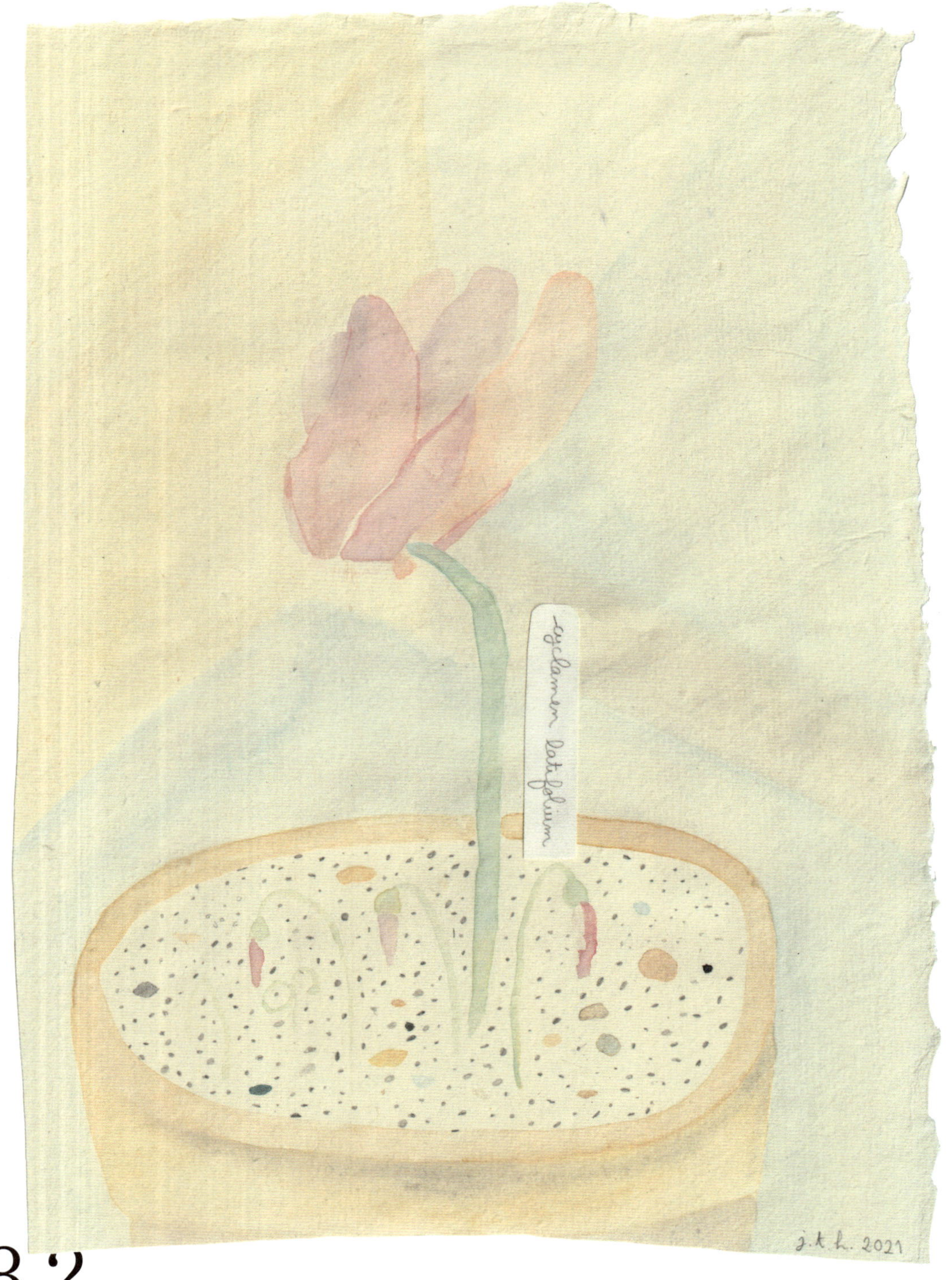

32

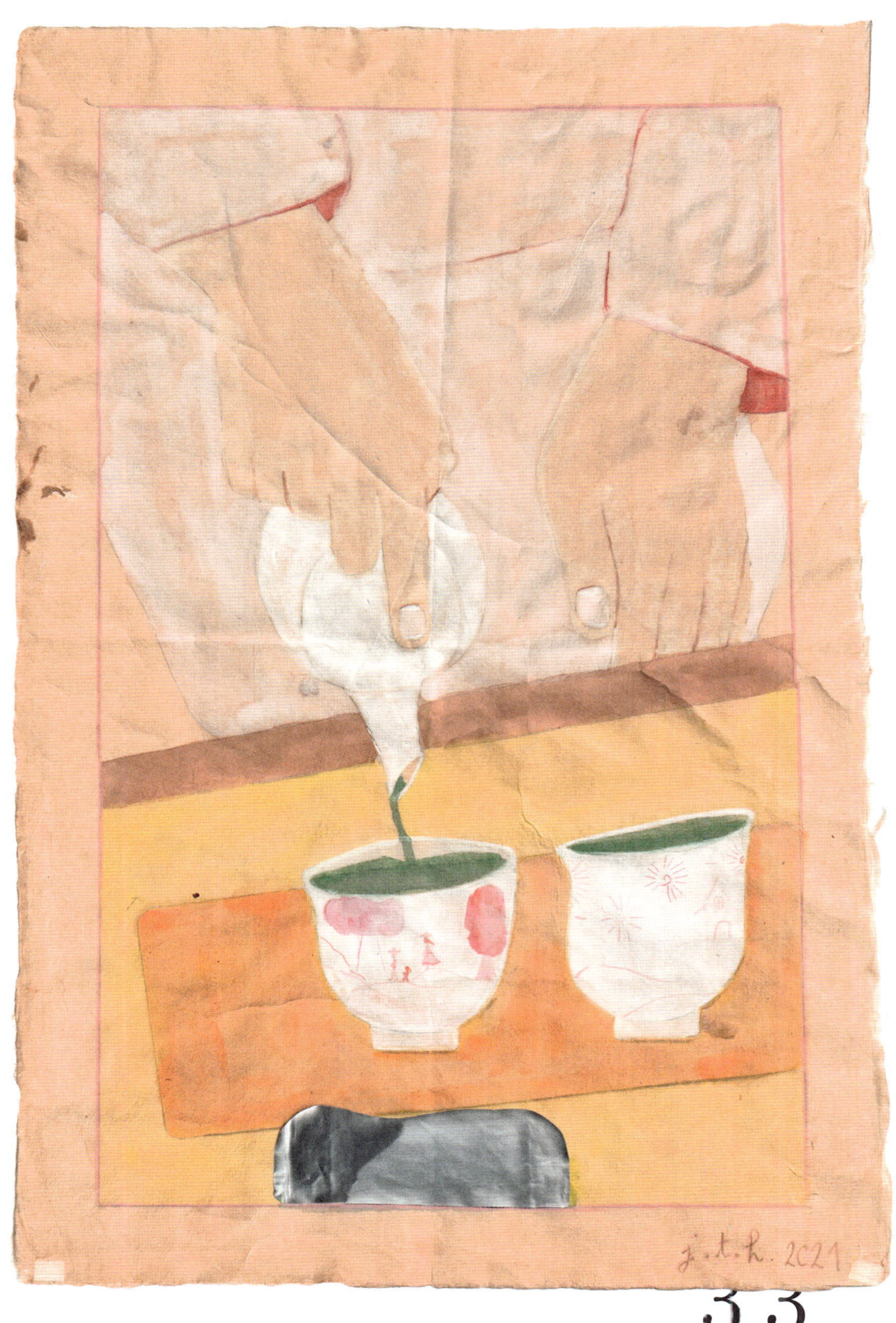

33

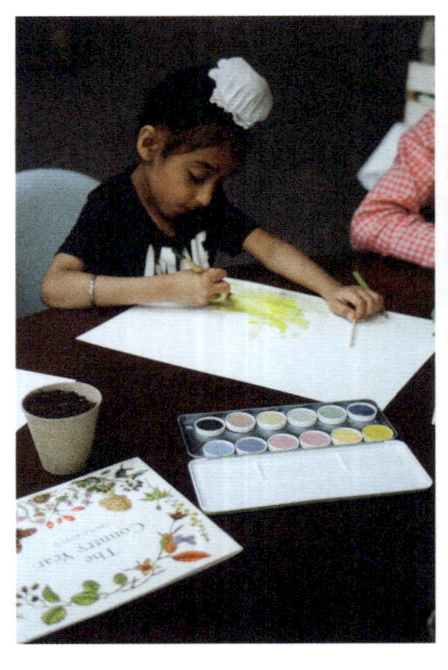
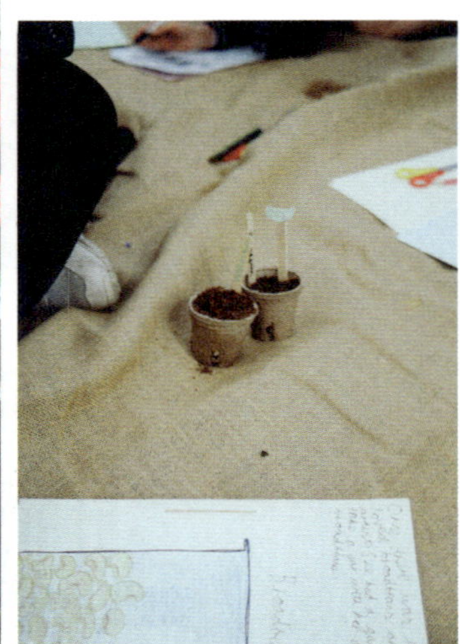
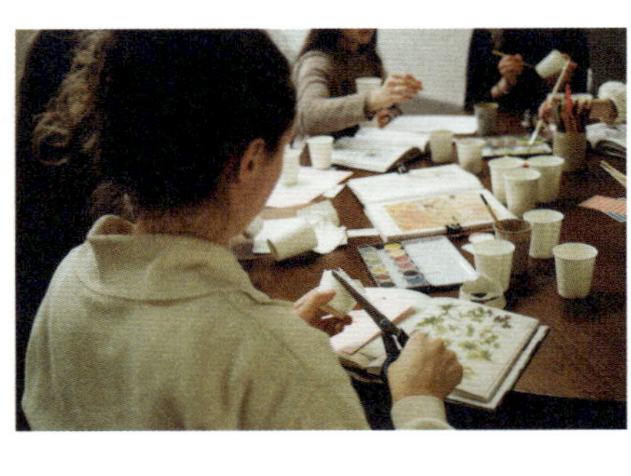
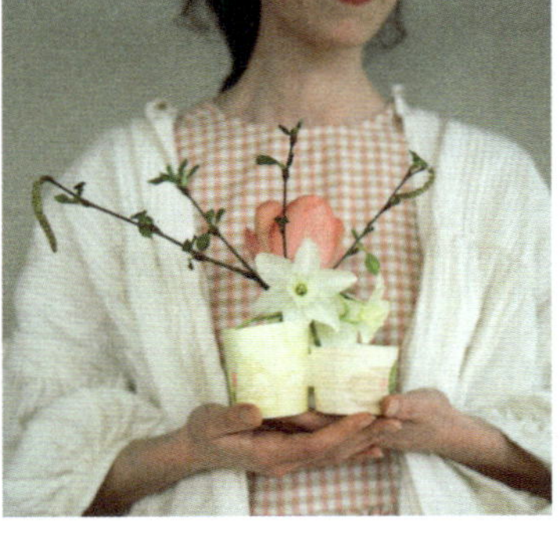
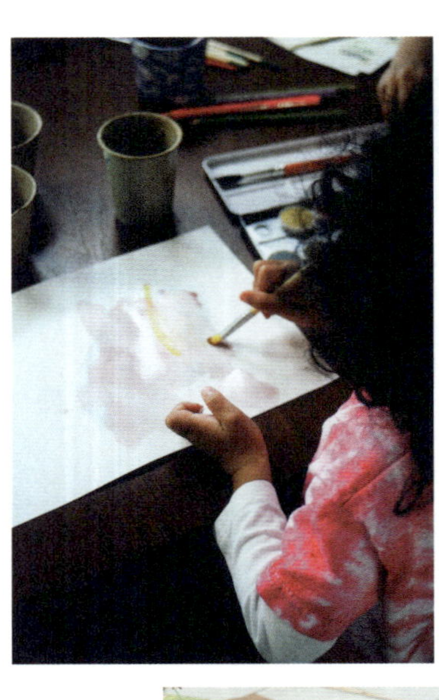
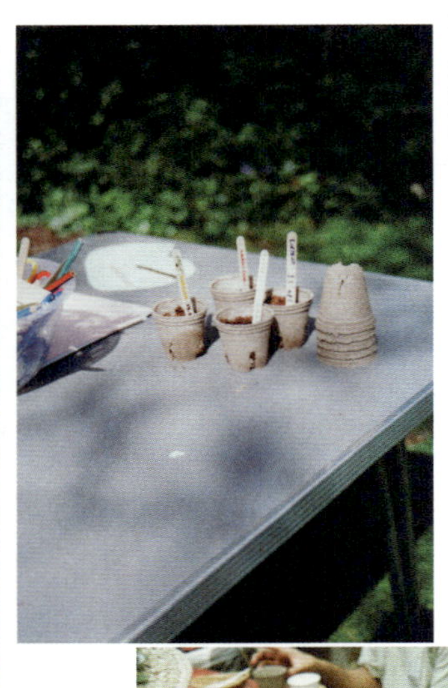
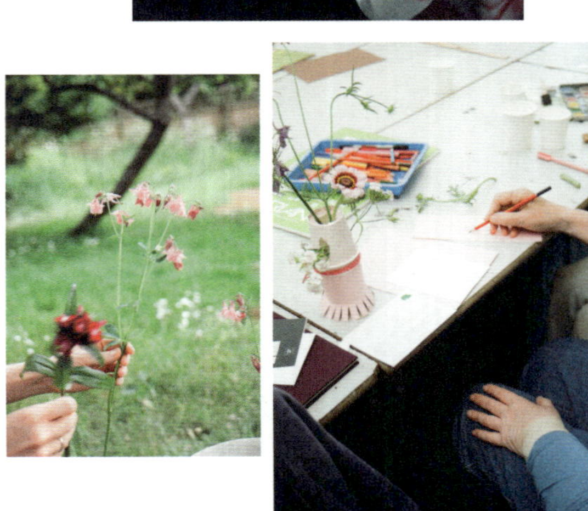
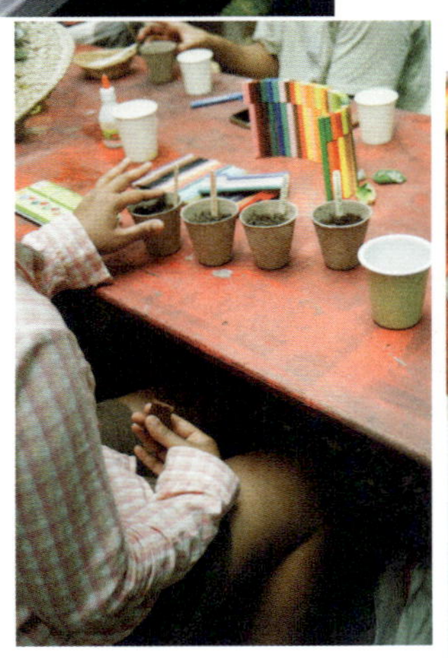
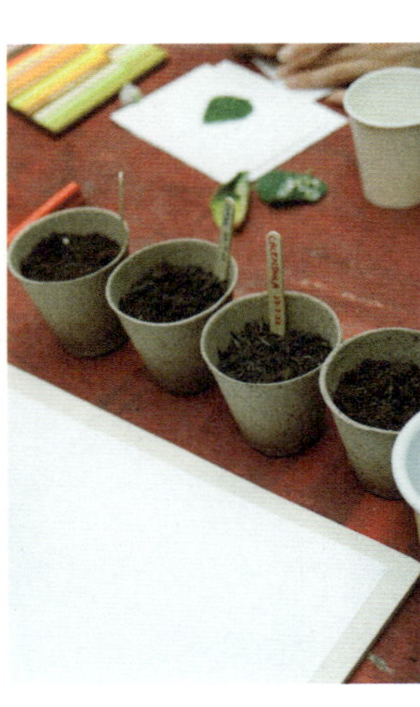

3 4

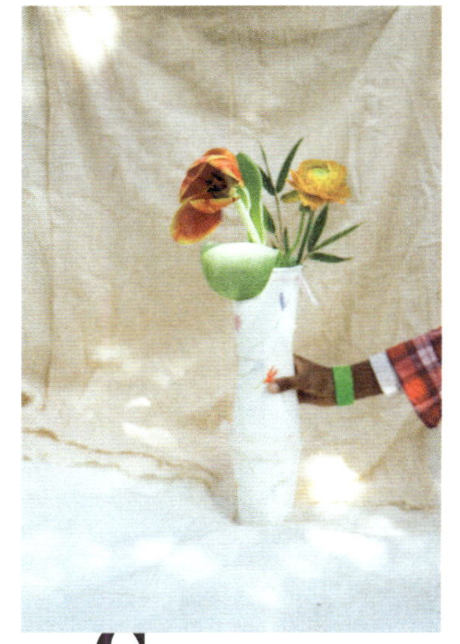

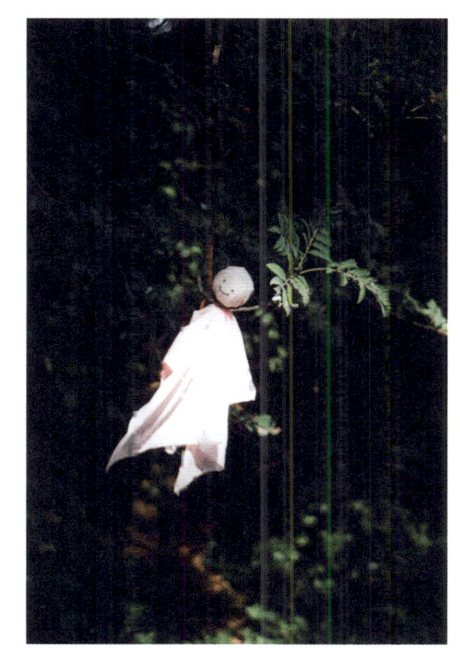

G
D
T C

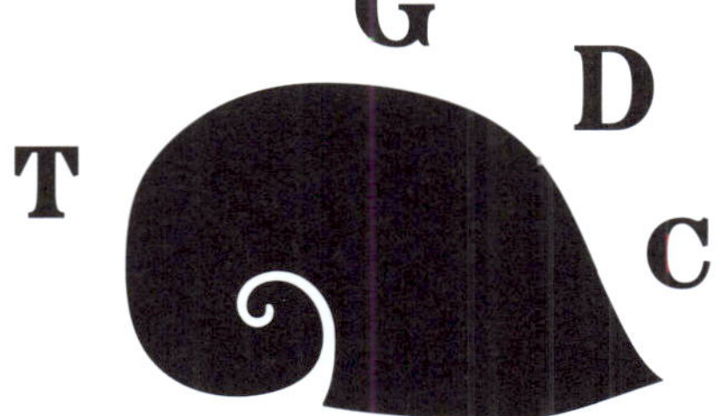

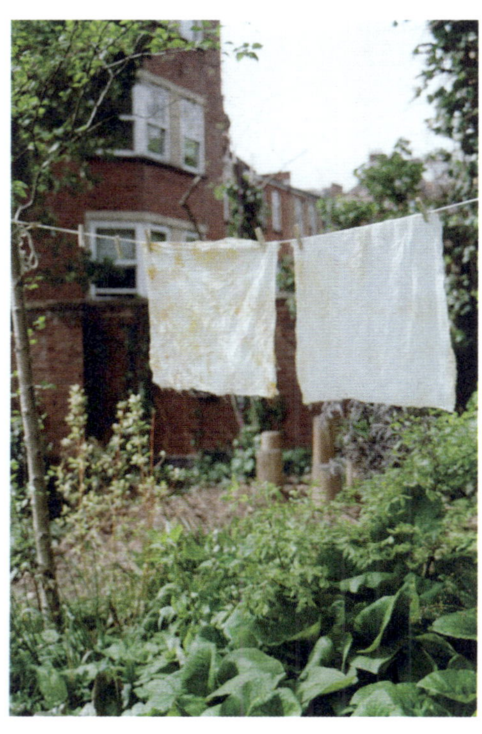

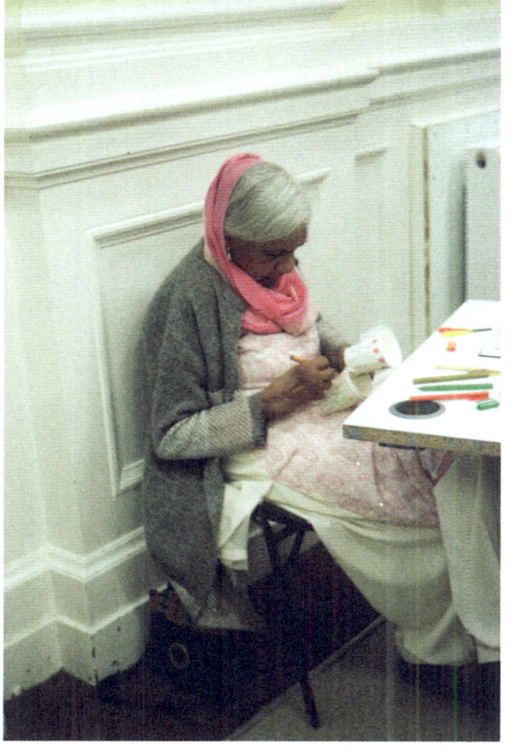

3 5

*Dreaming,
Remembering,
Building.*

Reflections on
Johanna Taga-
da Hoffbeck –
*Dreaming About
Tomorrow* at
Nidi Gallery,
Tokyo, October
2022

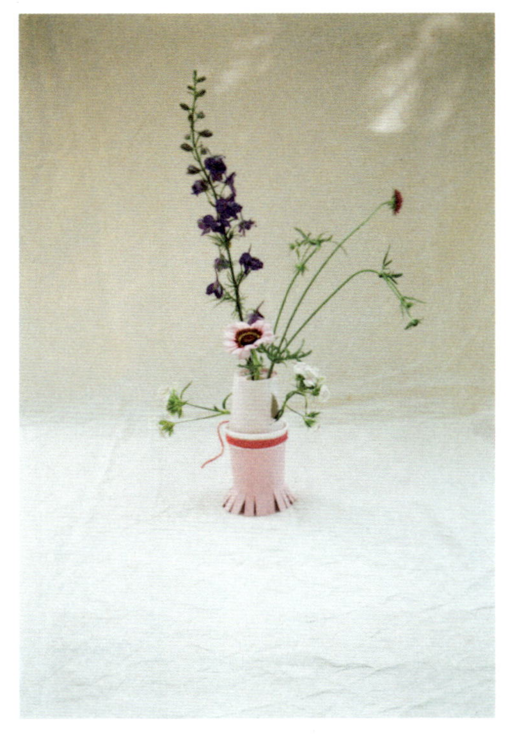

by Veronika Muchitsch

36

What does it mean to dream about tomorrow? Beautifully framing Johanna Tagada Hoffbeck's exhibition *Dreaming About Tomorrow* at Nidi Gallery in October 2022, the artist's introductory note articulates how dreaming about tomorrow can be an act of bravery. When stories, hopes, and lives end, how can we go on? In the face of death, symbolic and real, how can we continue to inhabit time? In *Dreaming About Tomorrow*, the answers to these questions are grounded in care, compassion, and community. Moreover, as I would like to suggest in this essay, the work of Johanna Tagada Hoffbeck (born 1990 in Strasbourg, France) entangles processes of imagination, daily practice, and memory, thereby grounding the future in the past and present. In the face of loss, it inspires to dream, to remember, and to be present.

Several works exhibited in *Dreaming About Tomorrow* bring into focus small rituals of everyday life, like the practice of preparing and drinking tea. This practice is illustrated in *Friendship Tea*, which centres the vibrant green colour of matcha tea poured from a teapot into two cups, and in a series of painted ceramic teacups created in collaboration with Olivia Fiddes. While depictions of everyday life have been a central theme in Johanna Tagada Hoffbeck's practice at large, in the context of this exhibition, they remind us of the potential smallness of the act of dreaming about tomorrow. In its attention to simple moments like a shared pot of tea, the artist's work offers a vision of the future altogether different from common narratives of acceleration and growth in the contexts of capitalism and the digitisation of everyday life. This quality also characterises four close-up photographs of flowers from the artist's *Analog Diary* series. Framed in broad wooden rounded frames reminiscent of airplane windows, the photos differ from visions of the future that may include bigger apartments, higher-paying jobs, or grander travel plans, and focalise what is nearby. To dream about tomorrow here articulates a sensibility of attention required for actively weaving the everyday fabric of time.

A second recurring motif in Johanna Tagada Hoffbeck's work, the depictions of plants, signal the continuously evolving role of horticultural practice in her art and life. In *Dreaming About Tomorrow*, this practice is also presented in *Broad Beans I*, *Broad Beans II* and *Outdoors*, three paintings each showing hands that plant seeds through careful gestures. Recently, Johanna Tagada Hoffbeck's dedication to caring for plants has inspired the activities of *The Gardening Drawing Club*, a series of community-based events of planting and drawing for children and adults, which the artist ideated in 2020 and initiated in 2022. It has also manifested in a special programme at Camden Art Centre in London that entails weekly gardening activities with primary school students during the academic year of 2022-2023. In these communal practices, the future is not only dreamt about, but actively built. Tomorrow thus becomes less a utopian vision than a formation that originates in deliberate acts of care, compassion, and community building today. Rather than a linear concept of time, these activities embody a multiple temporality, in which the future, the present and the past are continuously entangled and mutually shaped.

This dynamic and multiple sensi-

39

bility of temporality in Johanna Tagada Hoffbeck's practice reminds us of the work of French philosopher Henri Bergson. In his widely known volume *Matter and Memory* first published in 1896, Bergson emphasises the nonlinearity of time, and he conceptualises the relationships between past, present and future through his theory of duration. For Bergson, duration articulates an active understanding of memory, in which processes of remembering continuously tie the past to the present. In Johanna Tagada Hoffbeck's work, memories equally reverberate in the present and inspire the future. Through communal and cross-continental projects, like the free seed library that was included in this exhibition, the memory of the artist's paternal grandmother Yolande, with whom the artist shared the love for plants, informs present practice, and inspires communal visions of the

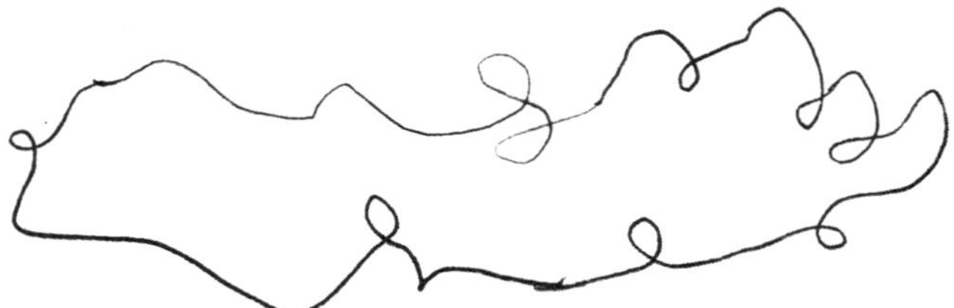

40

future.

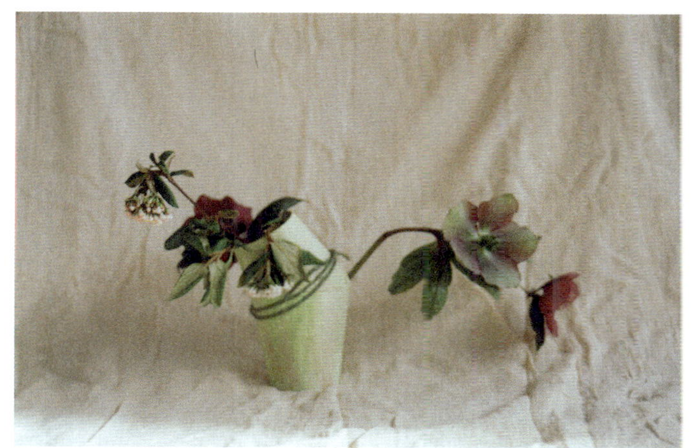

Dreaming About Tomorrow radiates with a radical soft-ness and unwavering open-ness that characterises Jo-hanna Tagada Hoffbeck's artistic and lived practice at large. As I have suggested in this essay, dreaming is here not an entirely utopian activ-ity, but materialises through actions of care, compassion, and community that weave an intricate fabric of time. In the face of endings, loss, and time standing still in small and big ways, this work in-spires us to dare to remember, to build the present and to dream of tomorrow, as blurry as it may appear.

41

List of Plates

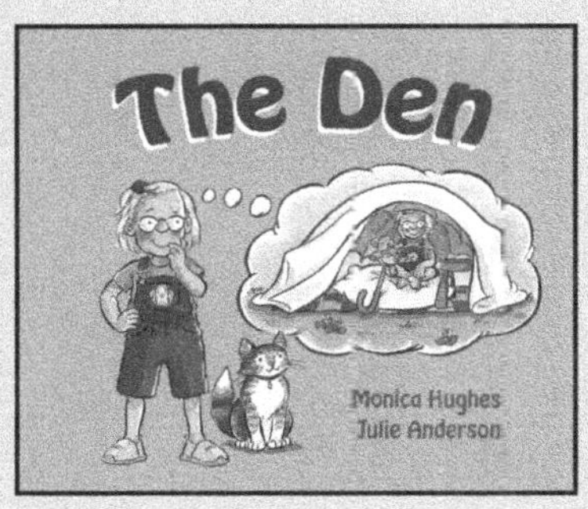

Walkthrough

Look at the picture.

Kim has an idea. What is she thinking about?

How do you know?

What do you think the story will be about?

Let's read the title together.

Has anybody here got a den?

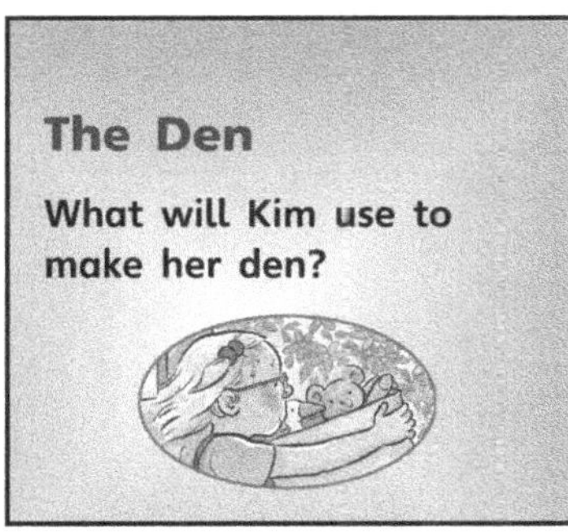

Walkthrough

This is the blurb. Let's read the blurb together.

'What will Kim use to make her den?'

(Prompt for suggestions.)

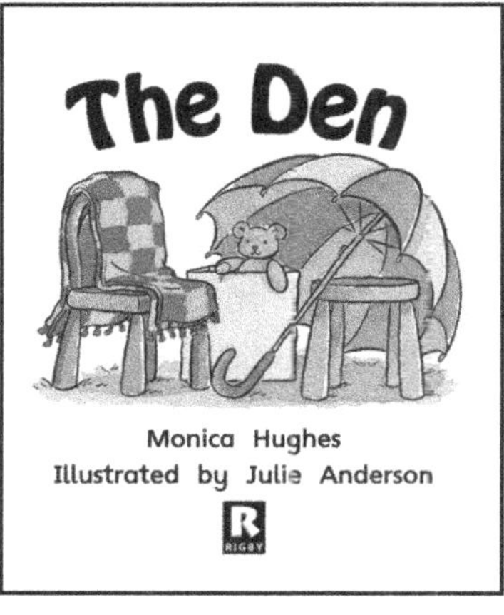

Walkthrough

This is the title page.

Let's re-read the title together.

Look at the picture.

What has Kim got to build her den?

These are the names of the author and illustrator.

1

Kim's collecting things for her den.

What does she get here?

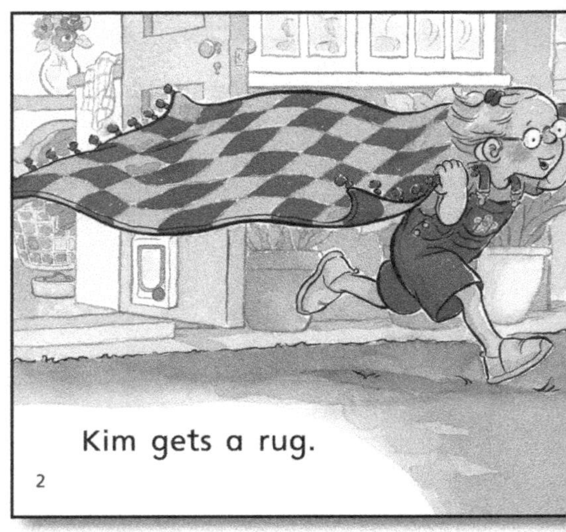

Observe and Prompt

Word Recognition

- Check the children are reading the CVC words 'Kim' and 'rug' using their decoding skills. Can they blend the sounds in these words?

- Check the children are using their decoding skills to read the CVCC word 'gets'. Ask them to sound and blend the phonemes g-e-t-s through the word.